A Souvenir
and Guide to
WAKEHURST PLACE

LONDON: HMSO

Seed head of giant Himalayan
lily (*Cardiocrinum giganteum*)

THE ROLE OF THE
ROYAL BOTANIC GARDENS, KEW

The mission of the Royal Botanic Gardens, Kew is to ensure better management of the Earth's environment by increasing knowledge and understanding of the plant kingdom - the basis of life on Earth.

Our mission will be achieved through worldwide research into plants and the ecosystem, publication, access to all knowledge so gained for the world's scientific community, and through the display and interpretation to the public of the collections at Kew and Wakehurst Place.

Whenever possible, the Royal Botanic Gardens will endeavour to reduce and reverse the rate of destruction of the world's plant species and their habitats.

In the countryside around Wakehurst Place, evidence in the form of charcoal remains and ironstone mining pits suggests that the area's wooded hillsides and deep valleys were inhabited by Iron Age peoples. Later, a Roman road ran through the estate connecting present-day Aldrington to Croydon.

The Wakehurst estate first appeared in recorded history in late Norman times. In 1590, the Mansion was built for Edward Culpeper and, although the building has been substantially altered since then, its imposing Tudor facade has been retained.

Few records remain to suggest what manner of garden, if any, surrounded the Mansion in Elizabethan times or in the succeeding centuries. Some of the larger exotic trees, such as the specimens of giant redwood (*Sequoiadendron giganteum*), clearly date from Victorian times and were probably planted by Lady Downshire (who owned the estate between 1869 and 1890). When the estate was purchased by Gerald Loder in 1902, the development of the garden came to the forefront. Loder was a passionate plantsman, subscribing to many of the plant-collecting expeditions being undertaken in the early years of this century, especially those to eastern Asia, where the world's richest temperate flora is found. With his interest in Southern Hemisphere plants, Loder also built up an outstanding collection of species from South America, Australia and New Zealand.

After Loder's death in 1936, the estate was purchased by Sir Henry Price, who maintained the momentum of the gardens' development. When Sir Henry died in 1963, he bequeathed the richly mature and widely admired gardens, together with a sizeable endowment, to the National Trust. In 1965, the Trust leased the estate to the Royal Botanic Gardens, Kew. The work accomplished over the last twenty-five years has transformed the gardens from a private estate into a modern, internationally important botanic garden. Wakehurst Place now functions as a 'green museum', mixing botanical science with the art of horticulture and highlighting the importance of plants for the perpetuation of life on our planet.

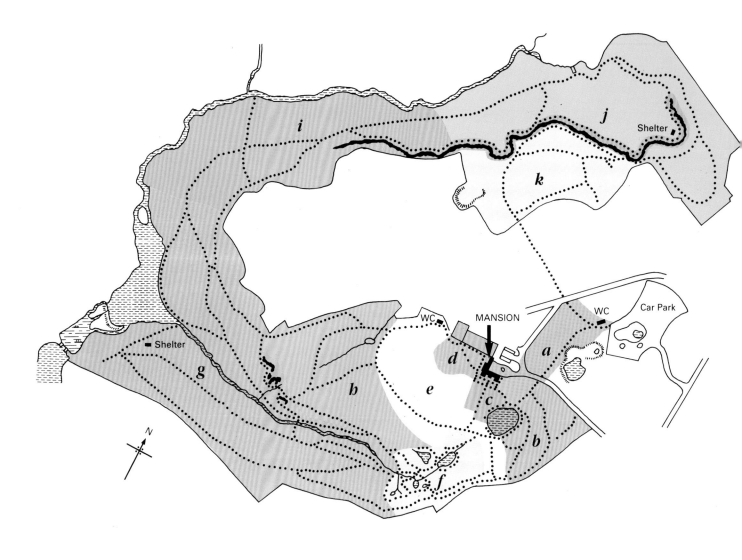

i

j

Shelter

k

a

WC

Car Park

WC

MANSION

d

e

c

b

b

g

Shelter

f

N

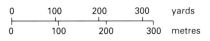

| 0 | 100 | 200 | 300 | yards |
| 0 | 100 | 200 | 300 | metres |

····· Footpaths

Rock Features

INTRODUCTION

Wakehurst Place, the country extension of the Royal Botanic Gardens, Kew, is situated amongst some of the finest scenery of the High Sussex Weald. Its equable climate, with ample rainfall and lack of temperature extremes, complemented by moisture-retentive soils, provides excellent conditions for the growth of temperate plants from around the world. Several important groups of plants, which cannot be successfully cultivated at Kew, flourish at Wakehurst, most notably rhododendrons and Southern hemisphere species.

The plants are laid out in a geographical arrangement that draws together plants from particular regions of the world. By way of example, one area of the gardens, Westwood Valley, has been reserved for Asian plants, whereas the plants of North America are held in Horsebridge Wood.

In addition to the exotic plantings for which Wakehurst Place is best known, the undisturbed nature of the woods and fields on the 202 ha estate provides habitats for all manner of mammals, birds and insects. Also to be seen are a great variety of native plants, including rare species such as the Tunbridge Wells filmy fern (*Hymenophyllum tunbridgense*) and the violet helleborine (*Epipactis purpurata*). In recognition of this, a large part of the estate has been designated a Site of Special Scientific Interest by the Nature Conservancy Council.

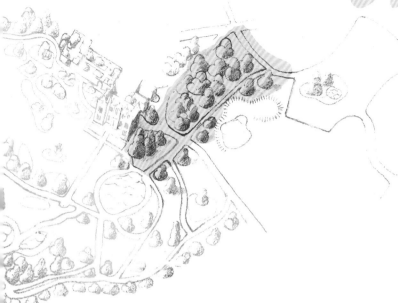

T he main path from the Entrance, which is situated at the highest part of the estate, leads down past trees and shrubs selected for their autumn colour. Particularly notable are various enkianthus and spindle-berries (*Euonymus*) with leaves that become flame red in October. In spring, drifts of naturalized daffodils (*Narcissus pseudonarcissus*) carpet the ground.

Closer to the Mansion, the right-hand fork of the path, flanked by huge specimens of giant redwood (*Sequoiadendron giganteum*), leads to the Carriage Ring. Displayed against the walls around this circular drive is a range of interesting plants, including the spring-flowering *Forsythia suspensa* and the familiar wisteria (*Wisteria sinensis*).

Above. Autumn foliage of
Euonymus alatus

Right. Giant redwoods,
Sequoiadendron giganteum

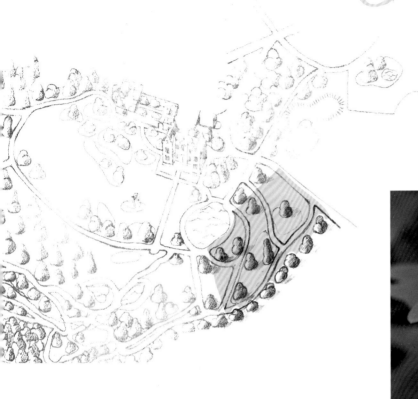

ROCK TERRACES AND
TRANS-ASIAN HEATH GARDEN

Beside the pond to the east of the Mansion are two interesting features. The Rock Terraces are a long-standing attraction that replaced a rock-garden previously on the same site. A wide range of dwarf and slow-growing plants, such as alpine forms of hypericums and potentillas, are complemented by mature specimens of Japanese maples (*Acer*) and other choice trees.

ROBERT FORTUNE

*Winter jasmine (**Jasminum nudiflorum**), bleeding heart (**Dicentra spectabilis**) and white wisteria (**Wisteria sinensis** 'Alba') are among the species introduced into cultivation in Britain by Robert Fortune (1812-1880). While employed by the East India Company, and later the American Government, to collect new tea (**Camellia sinensis**) varieties, Fortune made four expeditions to China between 1843 and 1859. He also visited the Philippines and Japan, which he described as more beautiful than any other country in springtime.*

In Fortune's time, travel in the Far East was very hazardous, particularly for Europeans, and he experienced shipwrecks and thieves. On one occasion he disguised himself as a Chinaman, complete with pigtail, to escape pursuing bandits.

Above. Autumn colour - *Acer japonicum*

Right. Drumstick primula, *Primula denticulata*

11

Left. *Rhododendron saluenense*

Below. 'Heath' rhododendrons growing at 3,600 m in north-western Yunnan, China

Below left. Cotoneaster berries

Right. Juniperus conferta

In contrast, the Trans-Asian Heath Garden is a much newer development, sited in what used to be the Rhododendron Walk. This area was so badly damaged by the storm of October 1987 that the landscape had to be totally redesigned. The loss of mature trees has created more exposed conditions that are ideal for the cultivation of 'heath' rhododendrons, dwarf species which grow above the tree-line in the mountains of eastern Asia. An impression of their typical habitat will be given by grouping these plants with gaultherias, cotoneasters, junipers and other species naturally associated with them in the wild.

12

FRANK KINGDON WARD

*A man of great patience, immense energy, resolution and endurance, Frank Kingdon Ward (1885-1958) travelled throughout the mountains of the eastern Himalaya in his search for beautiful and interesting plants. In the course of nearly 50 years collecting he discovered many species new to science. Amongst the plants he introduced into cultivation is the Himalayan blue poppy (**Meconopsis betonicifolia**).*

Kingdon Ward was a renowned field botanist, taking a great interest in the natural distribution and ecology of the plants he saw on his expeditions. He wrote over twenty five books and numerous scientific articles containing tales of his travels and experiences.

THE MANSION

Below. *Schizophragma integrifolium*

Right. The imposing Tudor facade of the Mansion

The magnificent Tudor house provides a focal point for the whole estate. Housed in the Mansion. are the gardens' offices and a visitor information centre, together with a shop and restaurant. Antique furniture is arranged in some rooms, recreating the appearance of the Mansion's interior when it was still a private house.

Behind the scenes in the Mansion are the Plant Physiology laboratories where seeds and their germination are studied. These are associated with the World Seed Bank, a cold dry room which holds seeds from over 1% of the world's species of flowering plant as a conservation and research resource.

Rambling over the walls of the Mansion are a variety of exotic climbers from all over the world, including the Chinese *Parthenocissus henryana* with its attractive patterned leaves and *Schizophragma integrifolium* with its large hydrangea-like inflorescences. The borders adjacent to the house are planted with various shrubs and herbaceous plants that blend attractively with the mellow Sussex sandstone of the building.

WINTER GARDEN, MONOCOTYLEDON BORDER AND WALLED GARDENS

On the western side of the Mansion lies the newly developed Winter Garden, designed to provide interest between December and March. Plants commonly grown for their winter colour are mixed with less well-known and more subtle species. The brightly coloured stems of various dogwoods (*Cornus*) and willows (*Salix*) contrast with dried leaves of the ornamental grasses, such as *Molinia caerulea* 'Variegata'.

Immediately to the north of the Winter Garden is the Monocotyledon Border, sheltered by warm south-facing walls. On the eastern side of the entrance into the Walled Garden, the border contains plants from the Northern Hemisphere. In the Southern Hemisphere border, on the opposite side of the entrance, South African plants are particularly well represented, late-flowering agapanthus and kniphofias providing impressive displays. Other tender plants displayed on these walls include the Australian daisy bush (*Olearia megalophylla*), with its spectacular masses of white flowers in early summer, and *Clematis phlebantha*, a rare and unusual species from West Nepal that flowers later in the season.

Above. *Clematis phlebantha*

Right. Coloured stems of common dogwood (*Cornus sanguinea*)

Far right. *Hedychium coccineum* 'Tara'

16

Left. Purple sage, *Salvia officinalis* 'Purpurascens'

Below. *Glandularia tenuifolia*

Right. Seventeenth century water cistern in the Sir Henry Price Garden

Hidden beyond the walls are two very different gardens. The main area is occupied by the Sir Henry Price Garden, a modern 'cottage garden' where informal groups of plants are arranged within a formal setting. Its restful atmosphere has been enhanced by limiting the plants to those with foliage and flowers in pastel shades. Grey- and silver-leaved artemisias and lavenders (*Lavandula*) present a subtle background to flowers of blue, lilac, pink and maroon. Particularly beautiful are the cupid's dart (*Catananche caerulea*) and various herbaceous clematis including *Clematis heracleifolia* and *C. davidiana*.

Below. *Salvia horminum* 'Pink Lady'

Right. *Artemisia* 'Powis Castle'

Below right. Yew (*Taxus baccata*) hedges enclose the Pleasaunce

The adjacent Pleasaunce contains a formal bedding area, centred around a pool and fountain. A clipped yew (*Taxus baccata*) hedge provides a backdrop for the unusual combinations of plants in the spring and summer displays. Outside the hedge, the borders have a more subtropical theme, using bold foliage plants and flamboyant flowering annuals. The surrounding walls support rare climbing shrubs such as the yellow-flowered honeysuckle (*Lonicera tragophylla*).

SOUTHERN HEMISPHERE
GARDEN AND SPECIMEN BEDS

etween the Winter Garden and the Pinetum lies the Southern Hemisphere Garden. Developed primarily by Gerald Loder between 1903 and 1936, this area contains many rare trees and shrubs, mainly from South America, Australia and New Zealand. Amongst the most striking plants are various members of the Proteaceae, including the Chilean fire tree (*Embothrium coccineum*) with its spectacular red flowers, as well as the telopeas and hakeas. At present, the area also contains plants from other continents, especially Asia, but these will be moved to fit in with the overall geographic arrangement of specimens.

Summer colour is the dominant theme of the Specimen Beds, an informal complex of shrub borders to the south and west of the Mansion which contain a wide range of late-flowering plants such as hydrangeas, potentillas and hypericums. Wakehurst's collection of hypericums has been designated a National Collection by the National Council for the Conservation of Plants and Gardens (NCCPG). This means that the gardens are responsible for assembling as comprehensive a collection of the species and cultivars as possible and making it available to other botanists and horticulturists.

Left. *Ozothamnus ledifolius* from Tasmania

Left. Chilean fire tree,
Embothrium coccineum

Above. *Rhodochiton
atrosanguinea* from Mexico

THE SLIPS AND WATER GARDEN

Below. Candelabra primula, *Primula bulleyana*

Right. The Bog Garden in spring

Below the balustrade in front of the Mansion, the Slips descend gently past mature specimens of magnolias, pieris and cornus. On the terraces of the Bog Garden is a rich mixture of marginal and aquatic plants which provide a colourful display, beginning in spring with various species of 'candelabra' primulas and ending in October with the robust beauty of the polygonums.

Below. *Polygonum affine* 'Superbum'

22

Close-by, enclosed by mature specimens of Japanese maples (*Acer*) and rhododendrons, is the smaller more intimate Water Garden, dominated by a waterfall. The central pond is a favourite haunt of moorhens (*Gallinula chloropus*), which often nest amongst the aquatic plants, notably the floating foliage of the water hawthorn (*Aponogeton distachyos*) and the emergent spires of golden club (*Orontium aquaticum*).

A flight of steps leads from the Water Garden to a damp woodland area, dominated in summer by the giant Himalayan lilies (*Cardiocrinum giganteum*), blue poppies (*Meconopsis betonicifolia*) and various primulas.

WESTWOOD VALLEY AND HIMALAYAN GLADE

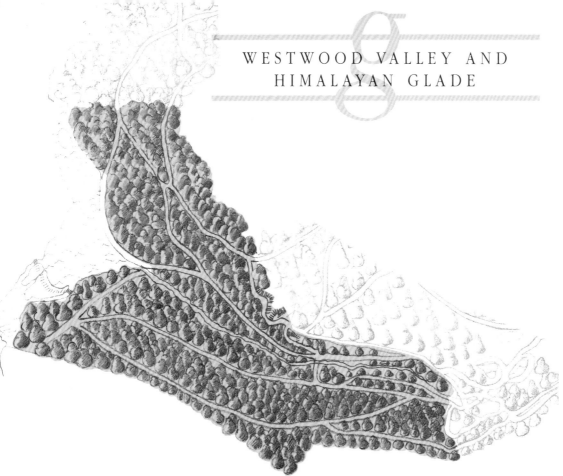

Below. Bluebells,
Hyacinthoides non-scriptus

Right. Looking down Westwood
Valley

The dramatic setting of the ravine-like Westwood Valley is home to the Asian collections. In its cool moist conditions, Asian trees and shrubs thrive, particularly the rhododendrons which provide a spectacular display from early spring to late summer. Complementing these exotics, the woodland floor is carpeted with bluebells (*Hyacinthoides non-scriptus*), lady's smock (*Cardamine pratensis*), common spotted orchid (*Dactylorhiza fuchsii*) and other colourful native plants.

Midway along the northern flank of Westwood Valley, in a deep cleft between huge outcrops of the underlying Ardingly sandstone, a Himalayan Glade has been created to show the vegetation of the mountains of the Himalaya and China. The main planting is of *Berberis wilsoniae*, a deciduous species with leaves that turn a flaming scarlet in autumn. Below the Glade, close to the stream running down the centre of the valley, is a bold display of polygonums and euphorbias together with choice ginger-lilies (*Hedychium*).

Far left. Hedychium densiflorum 'Stephen'

Left. Autumn leaves of *Berberis wilsoniae*

Right. Sandstone outcrop in the Himalayan Glade

TONY SCHILLING

Rarely does a plant collector get the opportunity to create a garden on a grand scale, giving to that garden both the plants he has collected and his knowledge of those plants in the wild. That rare event has happened at Wakehurst, where Tony Schilling has been responsible for the garden since 1967.

Tony's past work in the Himalayan regions, including China and Bhutan, and his recent experience of high-altitude rhododendrons, is reflected at Wakehurst Place. The Himalayan Glade and the new Trans-Asian Heath Garden are recreations of the landscapes he knows so well. Included in his many fine plant introductions are **Euphorbia schillingii**, **Populus glauca** *and* **Skimmia laureola** *var.* **multinerva.**

Far right. Sunlight through the trees of the Pinetum

The Pinetum stands on gently sloping ground above Westwood Valley. In the storm of October 1987, many of the area's 'champion' trees (the largest of their kind in the UK) were destroyed. However, some rare trees still remain, for example specimens of *Keteleeria davidiana* and *Taiwania cryptomerioides*. The ravages of the storm have provided an opportunity for an exciting replanting programme, allowing the collection of conifers to be arranged according to the geographic origins of the plants, with three divisions - Europe, North America and Asia.

DAVID DOUGLAS

*His taste for travel and tremendous enthusiasm for botanical exploration made David Douglas (1799-1834) an ideal choice as a plant collector. He travelled widely in North America, often experiencing great hardship, collecting plants for his patrons. Of the many new species that Douglas found, he is best remembered for the conifers he introduced into cultivation, notably Douglas fir (**Pseudotsuga menziesii**), giant fir (**Abies grandis**) and Sitka spruce (**Picea sitchensis**).*

In 1833 he went to Hawaii, where, despite poor health and failing eyesight, he continued hunting for new species. Tragically he was killed there, at the age of only 36, when he fell into a cattle trap and was gored by an enraged bullock.

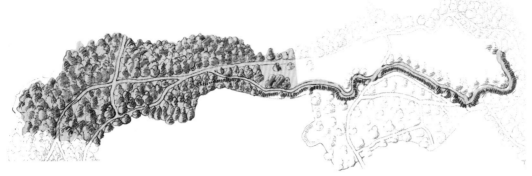

At the northern end of Westwood Lake, the footpath swings into Horsebridge Wood, where many of the North American tree collections are located. Here, as elsewhere on the estate, the storm caused severe damage and many trees were lost. However, as a result of the increased light levels, younger trees are growing fast to fill the space. Of particular interest are conifers from the mountains of western North America, where some of the world's tallest trees are found. Perhaps the best-known is the giant redwood (*Sequoiadendron giganteum*), large specimens of which can be seen throughout Horsebridge Wood. Plants raised from the seed of the famous old trees in California, 'General Sherman' and 'General Grant', have been planted out in this area.

Right. Bluebells (*Hyacinthoides non-scriptus*) in Horsebridge Wood

Below. Cones of the giant redwood (*Sequoiadendron giganteum*)

Running along the southern flank of Horsebridge Wood is a continuous outcrop of Ardingly sandstone, skirted by a path known as Rock Walk. The rocks support a unique range of moisture-sensitive native plants which are usually only found along the west coast of the British Isles. These plants can grow at Wakehurst Place because the humidity levels remain high in the enclosed valleys. There are many unusual mosses, liverworts, lichens and ferns, including the hay-scented buckler fern (*Dryopteris aemula*).

Above. Yew, *Taxus baccata*

Right. Exposed roots in Rock Walk, before the storm of October 1987

BLOOMER'S VALLEY AND COATES' WOOD

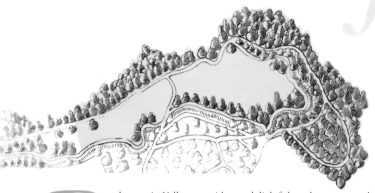

Below. Spirally arranged leaves of the monkey puzzle tree (*Araucaria araucana*)

Right. Looking towards the meadow in Bloomer's Valley from Horsebridge Wood

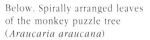

Bloomer's Valley provides a delightful and unexpected contrast to the wooded hills which surround it. It was planted with crops during the early and middle decades of this century, but has now been converted into a sweeping open meadow, maintained by frequent mowing. Fringing the north-western side of the valley are trees collected from Asia Minor whilst further to the north are many mature exotic trees including cedars (*Cedrus*), larches (*Larix*) and monkey-puzzle trees (*Araucaria araucana*). Above Bloomer's Valley lies Coates' Wood which holds Japanese and Southern Hemisphere trees as well as the NCCPG National Collection of southern beeches (*Nothofagus*), including *N. glauca*, *N. alpina* and other species rarely seen in cultivation.

Right. Shaggy ink cap, *Coprinus comatus*

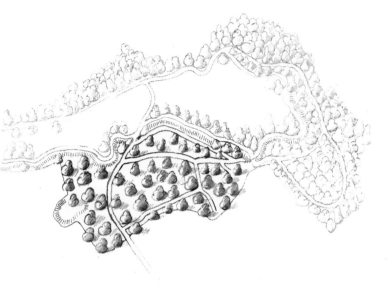

Right. Peeling bark on the Himalayan birch (*Betula utilis*)

Far right. Autumn foliage of *Betula alleghamensis*

S oon after the Royal Botanic Gardens, Kew, began managing the estate, the birch (*Betula*) collection was relocated to Wakehurst. These trees find the moisture-retentive soils and higher rainfall of the Weald more congenial than the drier conditions of Kew. Since then the birch collection in Bethlehem Wood has developed considerably and today it is recognized as the most comprehensive in the country. As the NCCPG National Collection, it is used by many gardeners and botanists alike. In common with the majority of the plants in the gardens, the birches are grouped geographically. In the central area are the Asian species, flanked on the south and west by their European counterparts, with the North American species occupying the remaining space.

THE LODER VALLEY RESERVE

Far left. A branch of the Ardingly reservoir runs through the Loder Valley Reserve

Left above. Elephant hawk moth (*Deilephia elpenor*) on rose bay willow-herb (*Chamerion angustifolium*)

Left below. Early purple orchid, *Orchis mascula*

Below. *Strobilomyces floccopus*

L ying on the south-western edge of the Wakehurst estate is the Loder Valley Reserve, an area of 48 ha dedicated to the conservation of the plants and animals of the Weald. The Reserve, which encompasses a branch of the Ardingly Reservoir, some 16 ha in size, contains a rich variety of habitats, including woodland, meadowland and wetlands.

In order to avoid undue disturbance to wildlife, entry to the reserve is by permit only and these can be obtained from the Administrator, Wakehurst Place, or from the Wakehurst Shop.